Usborne

Boy's colouring and sticker book

Contents
3 Farm
19 Castles
35 Trucks & Diggers

Illustrated by Cecilia Johansson, Dan Crisp,
Annalisa Sanmartino and Giulia Torelli

D1427454

Farm

There are tractors, cows, sheep and hens to colour in this part of the book. You'll find stickers to add to the pictures at the back.

In the farmyard

Barn

Trees

Tractor

Trailer

Bird

Gate

Butterflies

Flowers

5

Feeding the hens

Henhouse

Chicks

Hens

Eggs

Sun

Girl

Hens

Worm

7

In the fields

Cow

Calf

Sheepdog

Sheep

Bull

Mole

Lamb

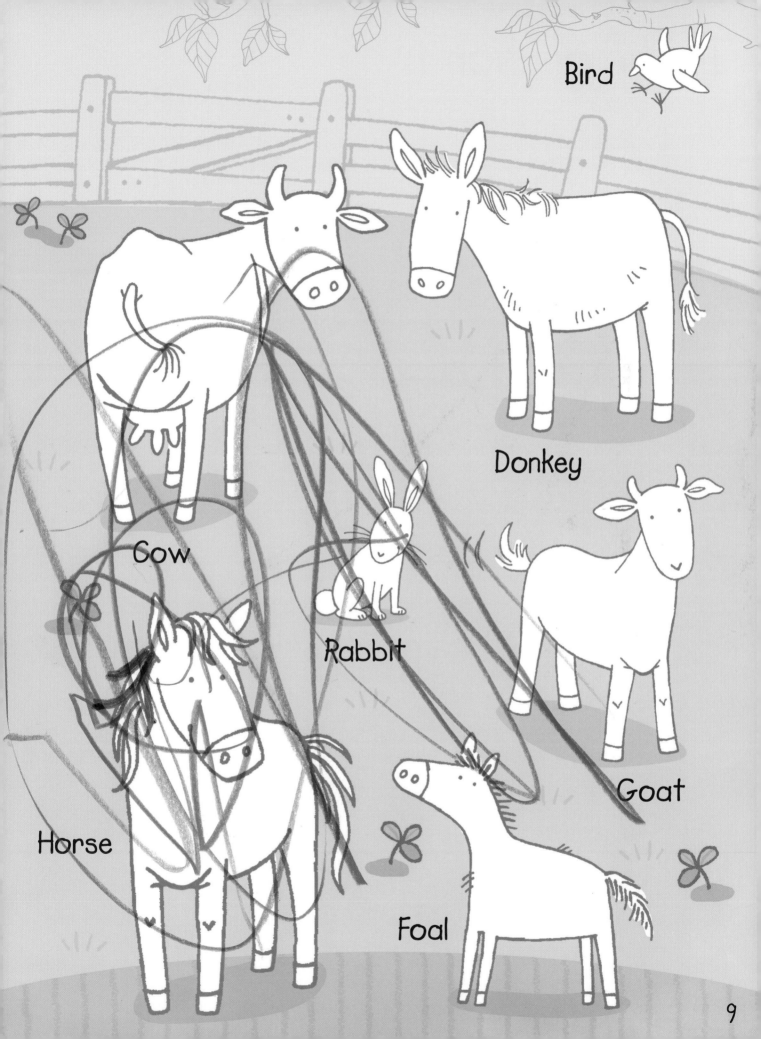

Bird

Donkey

Cow

Rabbit

Goat

Horse

Foal

9

In the orchard

Tree

Apple

Dog

Beehive

Bee

In the vegetable garden

Cat

Gate

Wall

Wheelbarrow

Rabbits

Cabbages

Carrots

At the pond

Ducks

Duckling

Frog

Duck

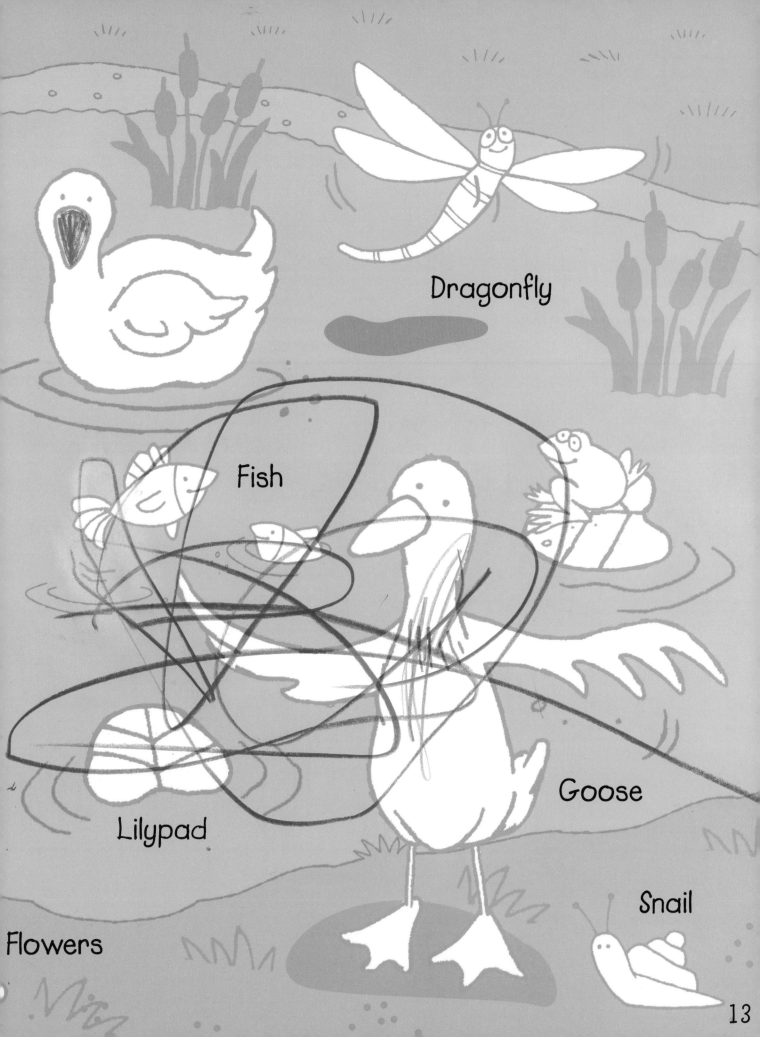

Dragonfly

Fish

Goose

Lilypad

Snail

Flowers

13

Harvest time

Crows

Scarecrow

Tractor

Mouse

Night-time

Star

Moon

Owl

Cows

Tree

Fox

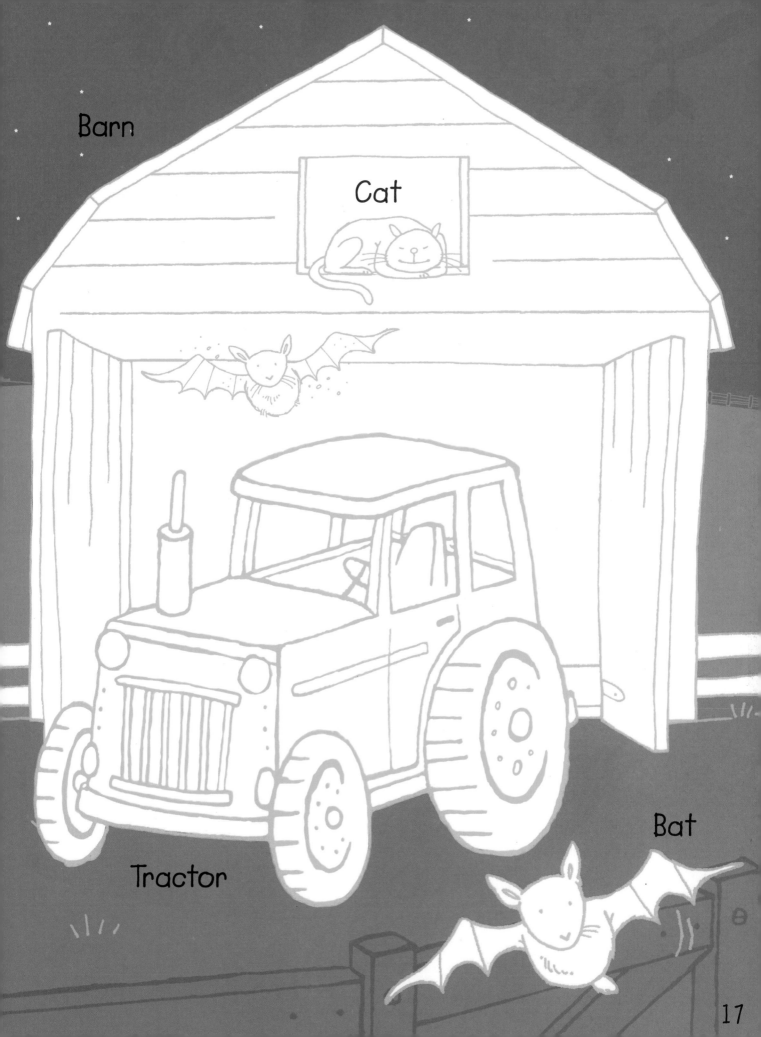

Barn

Cat

Bat

Tractor

Castles

Use the stickers at the back of the book
to fill all of the castle pictures in this section
with lots of jolly knights.

The castle

This is Brightstone Castle, where King Roger lives with his knights. Add more knights and ladies to the picture, and the king on his horse.

keeping an eye
out for enemies

The moat

The drawbridge can be raised
to keep the castle safe.

Keep out!

Now you're inside the castle and it's under attack. Stick the portcullis on to help keep the invaders out.

Stick two fighting knights on the steps.

Put some archers up
here on the ramparts.

23

Busy bailey

The bailey is a bustling yard inside the castle. Fill it with people and animals.

Find another horse for this stable.

A well, where people come to get their water

On the battlefield

The knights are fighting a battle to keep their enemies away from the castle. Fill the battlefield with charging knights, archers and foot soldiers.

This knight needs some help defending the castle!

27

Attack!

Now the knights are planning to attack this enemy castle. Can you help? They need a siege tower and a battering ram.

have put down planks
et across the moat.

At the feast

At home in his castle, King Roger is having a grand feast. Sit all the guests at the tables and give them some tasty food to eat.

The king wants music... find someone to play it.

31

Jousting

The knights are having a day of fun and games.
At the joust, two of them try to knock each
other off their horses. Add the charging
knights to the picture.

herald announces each
...ght before the joust.

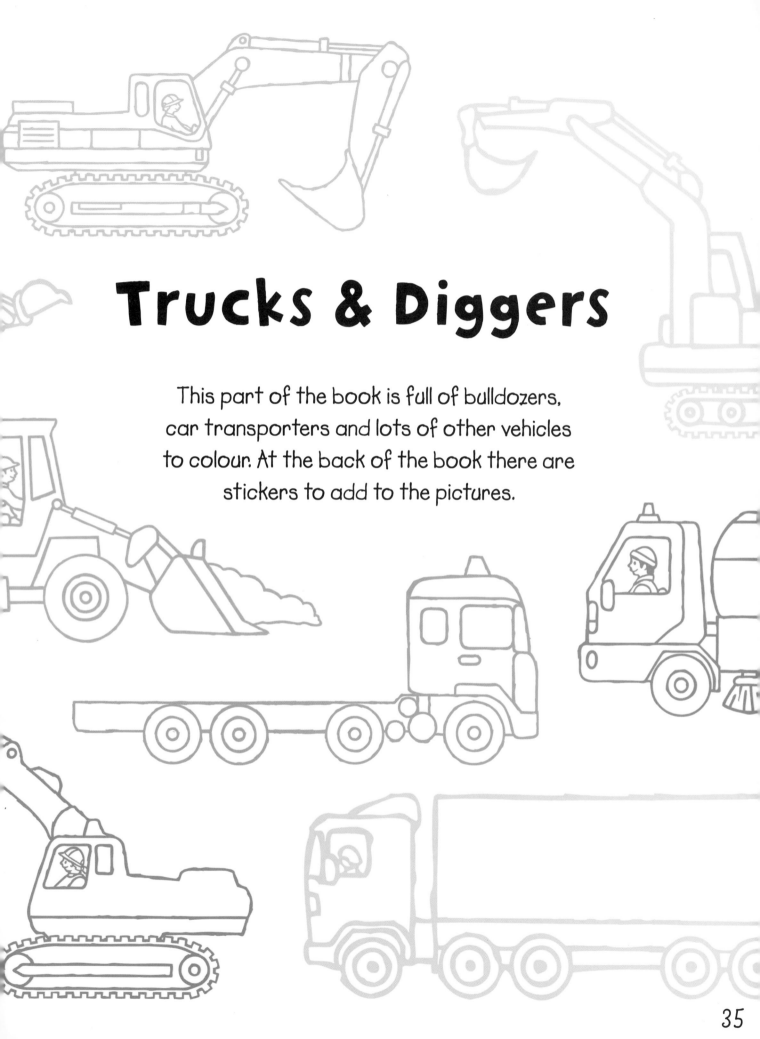

Trucks & Diggers

This part of the book is full of bulldozers, car transporters and lots of other vehicles to colour. At the back of the book there are stickers to add to the pictures.

Car transporter

Cleaning up rubbish

Street sweeper truck

Rubbish truck

Fire truck

Lots of diggers

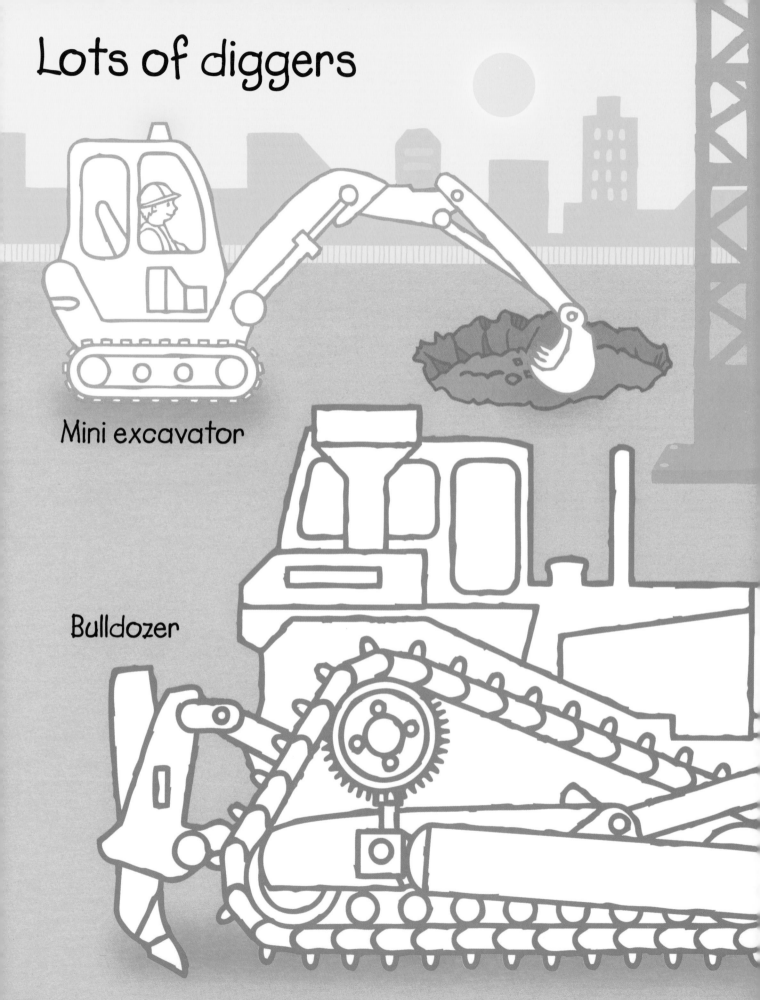

Mini excavator

Bulldozer

Excavator

Lots of trucks

Delivery truck

Van

Container truck

Dump truck

Rescue truck

45

At the building site

Excavator

Dump truck

Concrete mixer truck

On the farm

Milk

Milk truck

Tractor

Delivery truck

49

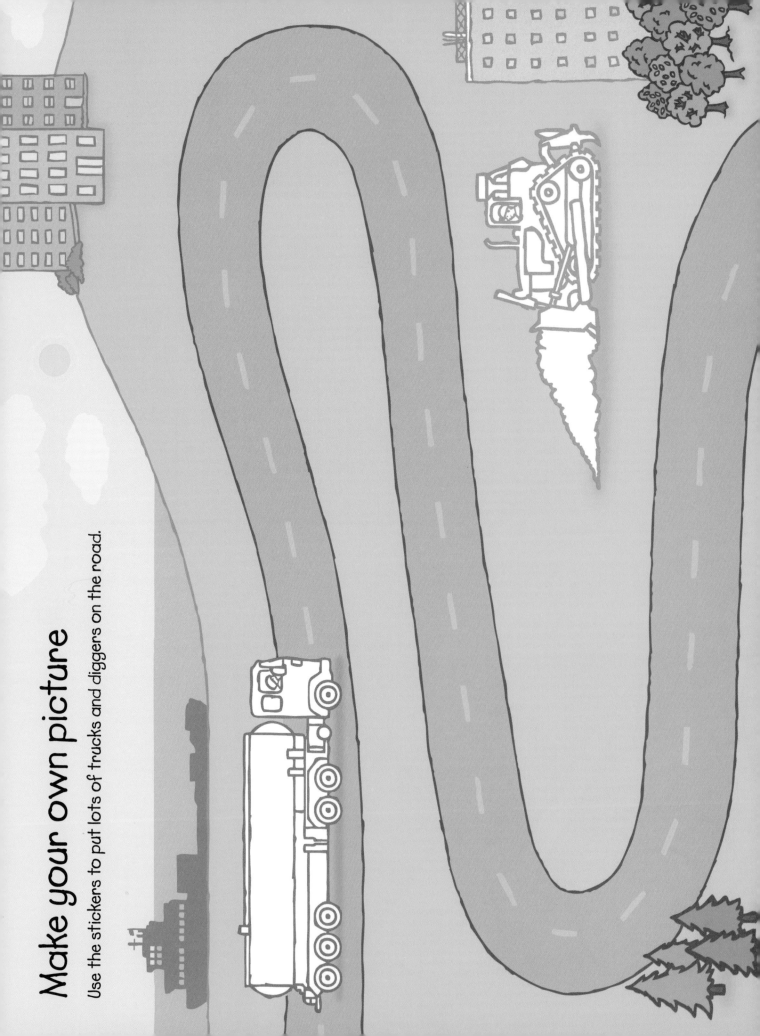

Make your own picture

Use the stickers to put lots of trucks and diggers on the road.